MY WORLD OF SCIENCE

Shiny and Dull

Revised and Updated

Angela Royston

www.heinemann.co.uk/library
Visit our website to find out more information about Heinemann Library books.

To order:
☎ Phone 44 (0) 1865 888066
▤ Send a fax to 44 (0) 1865 314091
▢ Visit the Heinemann Bookshop at www.heinemann.co.uk/library to browse our catalogue and order online.

First published in Great Britain by Heinemann Library,
Halley Court, Jordan Hill, Oxford OX2 8EJ, part
of Pearson Education. Heinemann is a registered
trademark of Pearson Education Ltd.

Editorial: Diyan Leake
Design: Joanna Hinton-Malivoire
Picture research: Melissa Allison and Mica Brancic
Production: Duncan Gilbert

Originated by Chroma Graphics (Overseas) Pte Ltd
Printed and bound in China by South China Printing
Co. Ltd

ISBN 978 0 431 13774 2 (hardback)
12 11 10 09 08
10 9 8 7 6 5 4 3 2 1

ISBN 978 0 431 13832 9 (paperback)
12 11 10 09 08
10 9 8 7 6 5 4 3 2 1

British Library Cataloguing in Publication Data
Royston, Angela
 Shiny and dull. – New ed. – (My world of science)
 1. Surfaces (Technology) – Optical properties –
 Juvenile literature
 I. Title
 620.1'1295

Acknowledgements
The publishers would like to thank the following
for permission to reproduce photographs: © Alamy
p. **23** (David J. Green - environment); © Corbis
(RF) p. **22**; © Getty Images p. **26** (Rob Brimson);
© Pearson Education Ltd p. **18** (Tudor Photography);
© Hulton Getty p. **19**; © Impact/Piers Cavendish p.
28; © Photodisc pp. **4, 17**; © Powerstock/Zefa p.
29; © Robert Harding p. **9**; © Science Photo Library
pp. **14** (Robin Scagell), **27** (Tim Hazael); © Shout
p. **15**; © Trevor Clifford pp. **5, 6, 7, 8, 10, 11, 16,
21, 24, 25**; © Trip pp. **12** (H. Rogers), **20** (Frank
Blackburn).

Cover photograph reproduced with permission of
© Getty Images (Stone/Chris Cheadle).

The publishers would like to thank Jon Bliss for his
assistance in the preparation of this book.

Every effort has been made to contact copyright
holders of any material reproduced in this book. Any
omissions will be rectified in subsequent printings if
notice is given to the publishers.

Contents

Any words appearing in the text in bold, **like this**, are explained in the glossary.

Shiny or dull?

Some things are shiny. A lot of light **reflects** off shiny things.

These bells are both very shiny.

Some things are dull. Although they may have bright colours, they are still dull. They do not reflect as much light as the shiny things.

Which is shinier?

The smoother something is, the shinier it is. The plastic **pepper grinder** in the picture is shiny. But the metal knob on top is smoother and shinier.

Some **materials** are shinier than others. All the things in the picture are shiny. Which is shinier – the wooden bowl or the silver paper? (Answer on page 31.)

Metals

Most things made of metal are smooth and shiny. But sometimes metals can be dull. Which of these metals is the dullest? (Answer on page 31.)

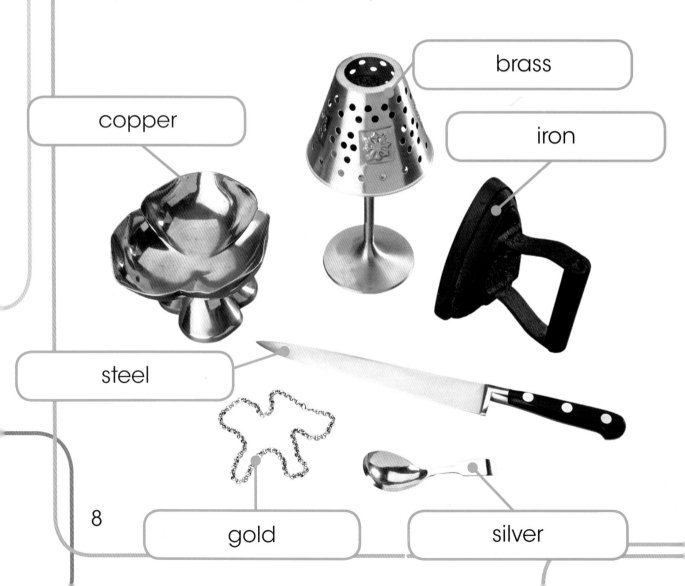

brass

copper

iron

steel

gold

silver

This toaster is very shiny. It is made of iron but it has been covered with a layer of **chrome**. Iron is a dull metal. Chrome makes the iron shiny.

Decorating with shiny things

Shiny things look more exciting than dull things. This is because shiny things **reflect** more light and attract attention.

These children are making decorations with shiny **tinsel** and silver balls.

Shiny things are also used to decorate clothes. This girl's scarf has shiny **sequins** on it. The boy's T-shirt has a shiny car on the front.

Reflecting light

Shiny things **gleam** because light **reflects** off them. This means that light bounces straight off them. When the Sun's rays hit them, they gleam like the Sun.

The smoother things are, the shinier they are. Dull things are slightly rough. Light bounces off them in many different directions. This makes them look dull.

This bicycle saddle is dull but the post it is attached to is shiny.

Reflecting light at night

cats' eyes

Shiny things can be useful at night. **Cats' eyes** in the road reflect the **headlights** of each car. They show the middle of the road ahead.

This man's jacket has shiny strips attached to it. The strips reflect the lights of cars and lorries. This helps drivers to see the man in the dark.

Mirrors

Some things are so shiny you can see yourself in them. You can see yourself in a mirror. The mirror **reflects** all the light straight back at you.

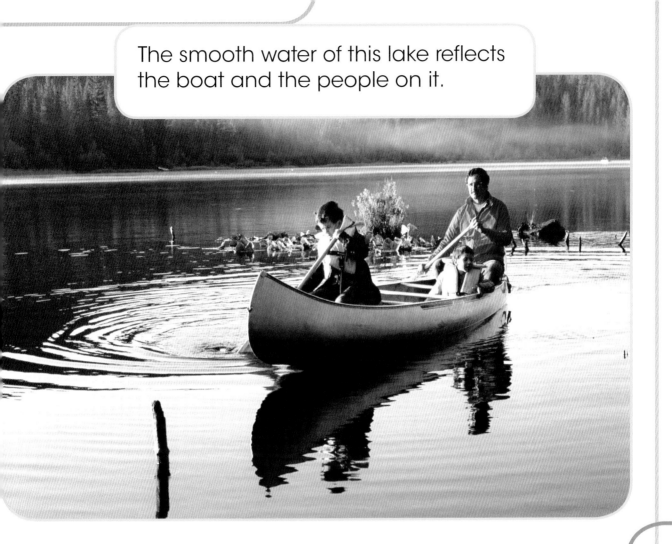

The smooth water of this lake reflects the boat and the people on it.

Very shiny metals can sometimes act like a mirror. When water is very smooth, it can act like a mirror, too.

Dull materials

These things are all dull. They are dull because they are slightly rough. They may feel smooth, but there are tiny bumps on their surface.

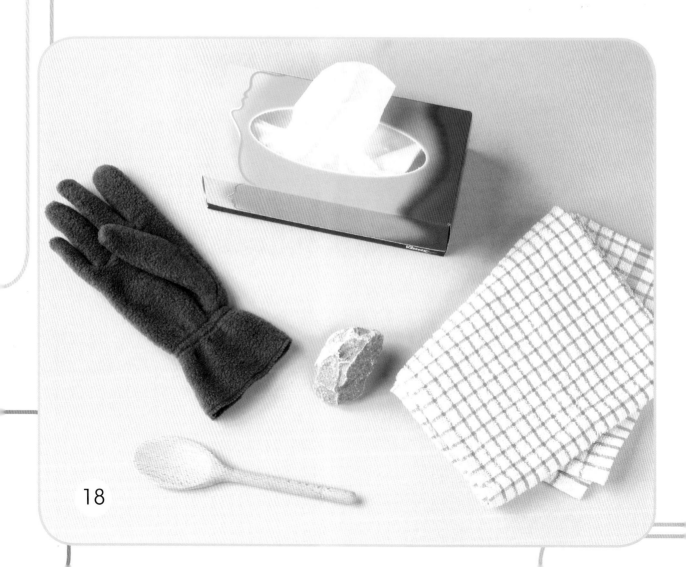

Many natural **materials** are dull. This house is built of dull wood. The roof has dull tiles on it. The trees are all dull, too.

Which is duller?

The mouse is duller than the wheat that it is on. Being dull helps the mouse to hide from birds and animals that would like to eat it.

The bag is duller than the lunch box. The jumper is the dullest thing in this photo. Which is duller – the spoon or the carton? (Answer on page 31.)

Dull can be useful

Roads are covered with dull, rough **tar**. The dullness stops light reflecting from the road into drivers' eyes. The roughness stops the cars from slipping.

Dull things do not stand out as much
as shiny things. Dustbins are dull so
they do not stand out and make
people look at them.

How shiny things become dull

Some metal things can become dull if they are not cleaned. The dirt stops them from shining. Iron things sometimes become **rusty**. This makes them become even duller.

Shoes can become dirty and dull. They have to be cleaned with special shoe cleaner. Leather shoes become shinier if you rub them with a cloth.

Making dull things shiny

This person is painting a car. The paint will make the car smooth and shiny. It will also keep out the rain. This will stop the car from going **rusty**.

This wood is being covered with a layer of **varnish**. The varnish will make the wood shinier. It will also protect it from water.

Polishing

Cars can become dirty and dull. People **polish** them to make them clean and shiny again.

Stones are usually very dull. Some are polished to make them smooth and shiny.

Glossary

cats' eyes small pieces of glass set in the road. The glass reflects light so car drivers can see the middle of the road.

chrome a kind of shiny metal that is used to cover iron and steel

gleam to shine

headlight one of the lights on the front of cars, trucks, and other vehicles

material stuff that things are made of

pepper grinder a small machine for grinding peppercorns into powder

polish make smooth and shiny by rubbing

reflect bounce off in one direction

rusty covered in a flaky, reddish-brown coating

sequin flat, shiny disc or spangle that is sewn onto clothes

tar black material used to make the top layer of many roads

tinsel short threads of shiny metal that are joined in a string

varnish liquid like a clear paint

Answers

Page 7 – The silver paper is shinier than the wooden bowl.

Page 8 – Iron is the dullest metal.

Page 21 – The carton is duller than the spoon.

More books to read

Is it Shiny or Dull? Victoria Parker (Heinemann Library, 2005)

Using Materials: How We Use Metal, Chris Oxlade (Raintree, 2004)

Using Materials: How We Use Silk, Carol Ballard (Raintree, 2004)

Index